from the Innovative Motivation Series
(Part of the *Music Motivation*® Series)

POETRy
THAT MOTIVATES

A poem is such a simple thing
it carries us upon its' wing.
We gain insight and experience true delight,
as we read each word from day to night.
Poems can inspire us and motivate us too,
and when we read words the teach and uplift us,
we learn, *and* know, *and then we* **do**!

JERALD SIMON

To my **sweetheart**, Zanny, with all my love.

Music Motivation®
http://musicmotivation.com

POETRY
THAT MOTIVATES

by JERALD SIMON

Music Motivation®, **http://musicmotivation.com**
P.O. Box 1000 Kaysville, UT 84037-1000 U.S.A.
info@musicmotivation.com; +1-801-444-5143

Copyright © 2020 by JERALD SIMON

For more promotional excerpt permission, contact:
Music Motivation®
P.O. Box 1000 Kaysville, UT 84037-1000
http://musicmotivation.com
info@musicmotivation.com

Motivation at its Best.

International Standard Book Numbers (ISBN)
Paperback - 978-1-948274-13-5
eBook - 978-1-948274-14-2
Audio Book Barcode - 191924596387
Library of Congress Control Number: 2020916717

Also available as an Audio Book, MP3 on iTunes, Amazon, CDBaby and all online music retailers. Visit your favorite online music retailer to download the MP3 audio book read by Jerald Simon.

Printed in the **United States of America**
Simon, Jerald
Jerald Simon's Poetry that Motivates by Jerald Simon Edited by Suzanne Simon

TABLE OF CONTENTS

Table of Contents

Table of Contents

About the Author (Music Mentor)

JERALD SIMON

https://www.musicmotivation.com
https://www.youtube.com/jeraldsimon
https://www.facebook.com/jeraldsimon
https://www.instagram.com/jeraldsimon
https://www.linkedin.com/in/jeraldsimon
https://www.twitter.com/jeraldsimon

"My purpose and mission in life is to motivate myself and others through my music and writing, to help others find their purpose and mission in life, and to teach values that encourage everyone everywhere to do and be their best."

- JERALD SIMON

First and foremost, Jerald is a husband to his beautiful wife, Zanny, and a father to his wonderful children. Jerald Simon is the founder of Music Motivation® and the creator of the Cool Songs Series (musicmotivation.com/coolsongs) and the Essential Piano Exercises Course (essentialpianoexercises.com). He is a composer, author, poet, and Music Mentor/piano teacher (primarily focusing his piano teaching on music theory, improvisation, composition, and arranging). Jerald loves spending time with his wife, Zanny, and their children. He enjoys music, teaching, speaking, performing, playing sports, exercising, reading, writing poetry and self help books, and gardening.

Poetry that Motivates

What is motivational poetry? Why did I decide to create an entire book of motivational/inspirational poems? Why should anyone read motivational/inspirational poetry in the first place?

This is actually my second motivational book of poems I have written and published. My first poetry book is titled, "The 'As If' Principle - Motivational Poetry," and features 222 motivational/inspirational poems I have written over the past 20 years. The majority of those poems, as well as many of these poems, were written for me personally. I often write poetry as a way to motivate myself to be better, to learn more, to express my shortcomings and weaknesses, and to write out how I plan to improve, progress, change, and see the world through new and improved eyes.

Many of the poems in this new book were written with my three wonderful children in mind. I wanted to speak to them and teach them.

The challenges we face today may differ entirely from the problems our parents, grandparents, and ancestors dealt with, and yet, everyone has problems that need solutions. That never changes. We all have good days and bad days. Everyone has trials, tribulations, struggles, and strife. Everyone has hopes, dreams, fears, frustrations, and everyone wants to be happy. No one is perfect and everyone makes mistakes, but everyone is doing the very best they can with what they have.

You can visit any distant plot of earth anywhere around the globe and you will find children laughing and playing together. Around the world, you will see family and friends smiling at each other and sharing memories, beloved family stories, and remembering the good times they have shared together while counting their blessings for having lived through difficult and trying times. We all experience excitement, enthusiasm, and pure adrenaline bursts of energy when we are living the good life and making the most of our precious moments here in mortality. We also know how depressing, dreary, and dark defeat and despair can be. We all have felt alive and on top of the world and we all have had times when we felt like giving up because for a while it seemed as though the world was collapsing all around us. We all have experienced our personal ups and downs. All people, regardless of size, gender, race, skin color, or beliefs are doing the best they can, but we all need help at times.

With these poems, I hope to lift those who feel as if they have fallen into a pit of despair. I hope to help those who feel hopeless and helpless - that they may, through the words of these poems, find hope, healing, harmony, and happiness.

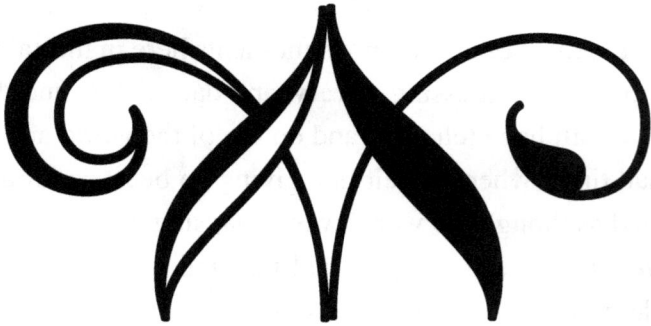

Take these words and make them your own. Read them silently
or out loud. The key is to internalize the meanings of the written
words - to take ownership of them and become a part of them as
they become part of you.

- JERALD SIMON

Befriend the Failure you Fear

Do not fear failure.
Befriend the failure you fear.
Failure can become a dear friend if you let it.
But most fear failure, and eventually regret it.

Failure is not a folly fool,
to be avoided, and dreaded, and cursed.
It is a gift we have been given so we might improve
the performance we've daily rehearsed.

Each step backwards is a friendly failure,
not a foe to be beaten and bruised.
For with each failure we learn something new,
though most feel discarded and used.

Do not let failure frighten you,
face it with faith and might.
Encourage it, and learn from it,
for each failure can bring you new light.

The Pursuit of Happiness

Be in the pursuit of happiness,
    seek it every day.
Look for it, and long for it,
    and live in a happy way.

The pursuit of happiness is a journey,
    it's not a place on a map you can find.
It is something you search for within your soul,
    an experience so profound, so simple, so kind.

Find ways to make others happy
    each and every day.
Do small acts of service -
    help others on their way.

We choose whether or not we pursue happiness,
    it's a choice we make each day.
Make a place for happiness in your heart
and then make a new start
    so you can live each day in a happy way!

Feast Upon the Words "I Can"

Be weary of the words "I won't,"
Be cautious of the words "I can't,"
 Carefully choose the words you use,
 the dos you do and the don'ts you don't.

Think about what you tell yourself -
 what you harbor as fear, guilt, or remorse.
For the words you tell your heart are real
 and can alter, at once, your entire life's course.

The words I can't and the words I won't
instill in one's self a firm belief.
They dictate what you do
and they become who you'll be.
"I can't," and "I won't,"
is what despair wants you to believe.

Focus on the words "I will."
Feast upon the words "I can."
 Believe in yourself and then create your plan.
Now follow it through
 and become a noble man.

There is More Than Life...

Happily welcome each problem and pain
knowing deep down there will be a refrain.
 The difficulties that arise and the trials that come
 will only continue until your life is done.

By that I mean there is more than life.
 More than the problems, and cares, and pain,
more than the struggles and tears and strife,
 more we can learn, experience, and gain.

Welcome each obstacle as an opportunity.
Learn as much as you can.
 Press forward with faith, and hope, and might,
 and look to God for His goodness and light.

Principles and Virtues
Must be Learned and Taught

I speak oft times of olden days
    even though I've never known such times.
Simpler times, some say they were,
    when you could always hear the church bell chimes.

Values and morals meant something then -
    principles and virtues were practiced and taught.
    Respect and reverence were earned and sought.

Simple times, some might say,
are what we need right now.
Instead of faith,
    fear screams and shouts.
Instead of hope,
    despair spits and spouts.

We need to return to the ways of olden days.
    Even though it seems we've lost such times.
Simpler times, we pray they were,
    when all the earth heard God's church bell chimes.

Values and morals still mean something now,
    principles and virtues must be practiced and taught
    Respect and reverence must be earned and sought.

Do not forget the olden days
    even though we've never known such times.
We need simpler times, as they once were
    when people listened to church bell chimes.

Why Do We Pity the Woman or Man?

Do we pity the man
who doesn't think he can -
    dream and set goals and improve?
Or do we work with him
and encourage him
    and help him get ready to move?

To move the mountains
    of discouragement and fear.
To overcome the obstacles
    of each trial and each tear.

Why do we pity the woman or man
who openly complains
but won't work out a plan?
Help them prepare for tomorrow,
to secure their success -
to continually do better
and to be their best!

The Seagull and the Eagle

The seagull and the eagle
   had a talk for an hour or two.
About their flights and what they each saw,
   but the two had an entirely different view.

The seagull flew low along the shore
searching for food and fun,
   while the eagle soared high up in the sky -
   over 10,000 feet high did he fly.

And what he saw from up above
strengthened his outlook
and encouraged him on -
while the seagull played games down below.

Do we live like seagulls
   and only search for fun?
Or do we soar like eagles
   and see the bigger picture of what can be done?

The Setting Sun and the Rising Moon

The setting sun and the rising moon
    crossed paths as they each went their way.
Neither one ever said much,
    and they each moved from day to day.

Years came and went and eons passed
    and neither one ever uttered a word.
From day to night or night to day,
    not one solitary sentence was heard.

The setting sun and the rising moon
    cross paths as they each go their way.
Much like the strangers unnoticed and alone
    who are heading home at the end of their day.

We must break the silence and utter a word
    to strangers we pass by each day.
For the sun will set and the moon will rise
    and then we are on our way.

Sons of Liberty

Knights of nobility and daughters of dignity,
rise up and faithfully stand.
For truth and right,
    for the noble and pure,
for the souls who feel lost,
    confused and unsure.

Be an example!
Be a light, a beacon,
    an outstretched hand
    to your friends in every land.

As knights of nobility and daughters of dignity,
your responsibility is solemn
    and your duty divine.
Your task is tremendous
    and your capability is sublime.

You can do anything you set your mind to,
    the entire world is at your command.
Be good, my noble children,
    it is time to rise up and stand.

Do Some Good

Do something good each day.
   Smile at a stranger or simply say hi.
Play games with small children
   or simply be kind to the people who pass by.

Every day you can do some good.
   Be it simple or small or grand.
In every way simply do what you know you should,
   it is time to rise up and stand.

So do something good and start today.
   Let goodness help you along.
Let this motto be your refrain,
   "Simply be good and forsake the wrong."

A Great Success!

I counted myself a great success
as I penned my little poem.
As I carefully wrote each little word
I felt, at once, at home.

Count Yourself Fortunate!

Count yourself fortunate when trials knock at your door.
Count it a blessing when hardships fall upon you.
Remember a time when you were confronted with pain
and think of the growth, the lessons you've learned
and the much more improved and fortunate you.

Fortunate are they who find joy in hard times
and savor the bad along with the good.
Fortunate are they who see potential in the rain
and are still kind and do what they know they should.

The Selfless Soul

Anger and Frustration
and Despair and Devastation
decided to feast on
selfishness and greed.

And the selfless soul
    who went about doing good
was confronted with criticism
    and was not understood.

Frustration and Anger
    were devastated in despair.
So they attempted to threaten,
    to frighten and said "Beware."

But the selfless soul
    who sought to do good
continued his course
    as he knew he should.

Help Me See With Clarity

I spake and the shadows listened.
I muttered and the meadows murmered around me
the thoughts that I have never before thought
and the feelings I've felt, but never set free.
You see, they encircle me and perplex me
and misguide me terribly so.

I need to be free of these fears I fear.
As a prisoner I'm bound like a captive in chains -
condemned, constrained, confined, restrained.
Release me. Free me. Please let me be.
Help me see with clarity.

Each Day a New Beginning

Be strong and be faithful.
  Be humble and take heart.
Each canvas a new beginning -
  each brush stroke, a new start.

Begin again, paint anew
the colors of the sky and sea.
Your black background
has become your matte -
paint over your past
for it never can last
beyond the present day.

Be wise and be virtuous
  be courageous and be true.
Each day a new beginning -
  each minute a new and better you.

Take Heart When Things Don't Go Your Way

Take heart, when your faith fails you,
and the world you knew crumbles down upon you.
Be at peace when your friends forget you,
and your own family actually derails you.

Sometimes fools can frolic,
    where the strong and wise won't go.
Often these become our leaders and teachers -
    they help us learn from our mistakes and grow.

So please, take heart, when things don't go your way.
Focus on what you can do, and do your best today.

Do All That You Should

I see too much of the living dead
who lifelessly wander around.
The vagrant gypsy who dares not dream
and the leader who lives life as a clown.

The lifeless souls of shattered men
who have been buried alive, time and again.
They once lived lives of prominence -
    but now they shuffle in shame.
They once were strong men, but now are weak -
    all that remains is their name.

But a name, in and of itself,
    does mean something and is of incredible worth -
regardless of the mistakes we have made.
    We all were born with greatness at birth.

Your name is noble.
    Your name is good.
Your name is integrity -
    do all that you should.

Your name is patience.
    Your name is truth.
Your name is possibility -
    be like the ambitious youth.

I've seen too much of the living dead,
   who have lifelessly wandered around.
But every soul who dares to dream,

    will at last, one day be found.

At the End of the Day

Tally up the marks you've made today,
   both the good and the bad and the unsure.
How do you think you fared today?
    Are you good and virtuous and pure?

No one lives a life free from mistakes,
   everyone stumbles and falls.
Everyone struggles and is bruised and scarred,
   heartache and frustration always calls.

So if, at the end of your imperfect day
   unpleasant marks have been hurled your way,
stand up tall and know you've done your best.
    That is all anyone can ever say.

A Towering Tree for Me

I planted a tiny seed one day,
in hopes that it would grow
into a towering tree just for me,
but the wind came along
and set my seed free.

I followed that seed across the street
and I watched it land at my neighbors feet.

Not knowing its worth or what it might be,
he stomped on my seed and buried it deep.
I slowly walked home and vowed to help that seed grow.
It would be my secret - no one else would know.

A year went by and my neighbor moved,
but I had secretly watered my hidden seed.
A seedling sprouted and began blossoming.
It only stood a mere foot tall, but it was overlooked by all.
A few years passed, as years often do,
and my little tree grew - oh, how it grew.
And then the leaves began budding, as leaves often do,
and I watched my tree do what all trees do.

It grew and it grew
and no one knew that I would shape and prune it.
I smiled when children climbed my tree,
and sorrowed when others would cut and scar it.

My tree and I both grew old,
as trees and all men do.
I often would talk to my tall, old friend,
and learn life lessons only he knew.

One day a storm came through my town
and nearly knocked my tall tree down.
Yet after the storm, I sat down with my friend,
and we discussed life from beginning to end.

The Non-Conformist

"Fall into line," they said to me,
"and be what we want everyone else to be."
"Don't have an opinion," they yelled at me,
"You can only see what we want you to see."

Too many, I'm afraid, go along with this game
and run around in circles all day.
Instead of originality, they fall into conformity,
and try to be what everyone wants them to be.

Everyone is unique! An original masterpiece.
Don't ever let anyone tell you you're not.
If you don't exactly fit the mold - that's okay!
Be good. Be true. Be honest and bold!

The Sorrow and the Pain

The sorrow and pain
   the love and disdain.
The sadness and gladness
   the embarrassment and shame.

The positives and the negatives
   the highs and the lows.
The good times and the bad times -
   the fasts and the slows.

Everyone has their ups
   and everyone has their downs.
It's all part of everyone's life,
   to live with the smiles and also the frowns.

Anything's Possible

Anything's possible and anyone can improve,
it does not matter what wrongs you've wrought,
what shadows of darkness encircle your soul
or the battles you've already fought.

Night may befall you
but the sun will continue to rise.
Despair may attempt to attack and destroy you
but don't listen when darkness tells you its lies.

Focus on faith and be positive,
even if others are afraid and hide.
Imagine a solution and be creative,
and in the end you'll know you've tried.

The Promise of Success

You have knowledge,
you have a brain.
You have potential
written into your name.

You have power.
You have strength.
You have abundance
and will yet partake:

Of the promise of success
of the dream of things to come,
of the beauty of tomorrow,
of all you'll do and won't leave undone.

Children Dream of Many Things

Little children often dream of many things -
of fairies and flying and kites with strings.
Of flowers and forests and the ocean shore
of one thousand and one fancies of which they never will bore.

As children grow older their dreams often change.
No longer satisfied with flying and kites and strings,
they set their sights on "grander" things.
They long to succeed, to accomplish, and grow.
They ponder and work and learn and know
a little about life and a lot about pain -
from the day-to-day struggles of loss and gain.

These children become adults with work and life.
They hustle about dealing with heartache and strife -
and the troublesome times that always come -
to the many who worry, and not just the some.
Life takes its toll and these souls tire soon
while their children grow older and hum a new tune.

As mature adults, aged by time,
their minds return to simpler times.

And these grown up children dream of many things -
of fairies and flying and kites with strings.
Of flowers and forests and the ocean shore
of one thousand and one fancies of which they never will bore.

They urge their children and their children's children
to fly with fairies and dream of things.
But most do not listen and most do not care,
for they have given up on flying and kites with strings.

Children, please listen and hear my hopeful words.
Fairies do exist - just ask the birds.
Follow your dreams and open your heart.
You can accomplish anything - if you simply start.
Begin and do, finish and follow through.

Children of all ages, please dream of many things -
of fairies and flying and kites with strings.
Of flowers and forests and the ocean shore
of one thousand and one fancies of which you never will bore.

Once in a While

Once in a while there is born a man
    who is stalwart and true and honest and good.
This man is determined to do his best,
    to accomplish all that he hopes he could.

But setbacks deter him
    and the unknown becomes known
and trials arise
    and the man feels alone.

Once in a while trials make the man
    who is tested and tried and must prove he's good.
Though he's fallen before, the man arises once more,
    to accomplish all that he knows he should.

If setbacks deter you
    and all you've known becomes unknown -
let determination help you do your best
    that you may know you are never alone.

Wrongly Accused

I was wrongly accused and condemed
    for something I did not do.
My name was marred - my reputation defamed
    and what was said about me is completely untrue.

Others spoke behind my back
    and whispered lies about me.
Friends and neighbors began their attack
    but I knew they truly could not see.

Yes, they had sight, but were somehow blind.
    They had ears but could not hear.
They were consumed by themselves and loyal to their lies,
    and in truth, were entirely filled with fear.

But still, I do not judge them.
    I love them and will pray for their good.
It is not my place to be cruel or condemn.
    In life I must do what I know God would.

Be Prepared...
Before it is Too Late

I look in the past
and often reflect
how the world was.
I live in the present
and often inspect
how my world is.
I dream of the future
and often respect
where my past and present may take me.
Diverging paths that
intersect and connect -
Prepare me for my future fate.
But I must hurry
and be prepared
before it is too late.

Courage Called to Me

Loneliness befriended me,
but soon left me all alone.
So I wandered for ages,
and lived life on my own.

Emptiness engulfed me
then discarded my disconsolate soul.
So now I feast upon my famine
and though deprived, I feel quite whole.

Sadness and sorrow summoned me,
bitterness beckoned me home.
Anger and hostility harrassed me.
yet they all soon left me alone.

I was abandoned
but I stood on my own.
And in standing I gained an inner strength
even though I felt completely alone.

Courage soon called out to me,
and my newfound strength supported me.
Then happiness delightfully held me,
and my growing faith set me free.

Man Seldom Finds

I gather that man seldom finds
the hidden treasures of mankind
    and diamonds, sapphires, pearls, and gold
    are tempting tales for the young and old.

Searching for cities that have long been lost -
looking for legends, treasure map hunting,
sunken ship diving, and soul-seeking searches.

But what have I actually found thus far?

Treasures 'tis true, but not what you'd think I'd find.
My most valued treasures are found in my children's eyes.
    As I see them sparkle and glow and shine,
    I thank God these precious gifts are mine.

Condemned for Being Myself

I had a dream the other night
a surreal and unimaginable insight.
   It wasn't the regular floating dream
   or even a thriller or nightmare or scary scream.

I dreamt I was summoned to a court room last night -
   to be judged by a jury of three.
I was condemned for being myself,
   by the man I longed to be.

I was prosecuted by my problematic past.
   I was forewarned and judged by the future me.
I was scrutinized and criticized by my present predicament
   until, at last, I was forgiven by my eternal me.

Follow Me!

Follow me when the dream is young,
  and the day is dawning and new.
Follow me when the first sunbeam shines
  and the sky turns from black to blue.

A heavenly hope hangs over my head
  like a blessing bestowed from a patriarch's hand.
And I know that in life I am being led,
  as I travel across this great new land.

So follow me, friend, as I follow God -
  where He leads me, I will go and I will do.
I will listen and learn and navigate each turn,
  and always live life anew.

Never Stop Trying

Never give up on the wounded soul
who's lost interest to live, who's abandoned his course
who's given up on himself
and feels no remorse.

Never stop trying to teach and inspire,
to motivate and encourage,
to prompt and to prod,
to reassure one another
that you're each loved by God.

Never be embarrassed
to show emotion, to cry,
to be human, to make mistakes,
to fail at something you try.

Never stop trying
to reach for the good,
to progress, to improve,
to do all that you should.

Never stop trying
to listen and learn.
In life most are given
what they deservedly earn.

Wait For Me

"Wait for me," were the words she whispered,
   to the young boy who held her hand.
She had work to do and went on her way,
   but the boy stayed there at her command.

"Wait for me," were the words he hollered,
   as that young man went off to war.
She had plenty to do till the war was through,
   but longed for the young man to return home once more.

Time passed by and the years marched on.
   The man returned and embraced his true love.
The couple wed and their life began.
   They felt God's blessings from up above.

The years rolled forward and children came,
   their family grew and blossomed anew.
They experienced the good times and the bad times the same,
   and this family learned lessons, from which they all grew.

At 92, his sweet wife died,
   and left the world he knew.
But before she left, she whispered these words -
   I'll be waiting, my love, for you.

The Inner World of Being

The Inner World of Being,
    is a place of sweet content.
Where dreams dwell and faith endures
    and the labors of virtue are spent.

This Inner World of Being,
is a very sacred abode -
    where the humble dwell and the meek abide,
    where all may flourish and peacefully reside.

I often retreat to my inner world
where I may perfectly be who I am.
    Where it does not matter what is said and done
    for I know the intents and hearts of everyone.

Our Weakness Within

Men are strong.
Men are brave.
Men are born free
but quickly enslaved -

to their habits,
    to each thought,
to their successes,
    and to the battles they've fought.

Their failures, their pain,
    their embarrasment and shame.
From the deeds they do,
    to the wrongs they do, but never name.

Men are enslaved
    by the lives they lead,
by their ambitions, by their shortcomings,
    by their endeavors and greed.

The strength men have
    and their weakness within,
combat and collide -
    they end and begin.

Strength and weakness are within each man -
the power to do, the potential to become,
the greatness we hold and the knowledge we can.
Such is the life of every child, woman, and man.

Impatience

Patience became impatient
    when reverence irreverently roared.
Kindness became uncharacteristically unkind,
    as the wingless creature suddenly soared.

Apathy and hysteria
    hackled and hurled their insults.
Chaos and commotion erupted and burst -
    for that wingless creature had its desired results.

The devil laughs and scorns mankind.
He tempts us to stray and wander.
    He wants us to fail and fall and cry,
    and often we follow him and then ask why.

The Unknown

We fight a foe we cannot see
who lurks beneath our skin.
The demon within,
the fiend who fights
against what we know is true and right.

The unknown within us
is the one we fear the most.
The monster we've hidden,
    the stranger we despise
the one who is continually
    feeding us lies.

There is an unknown around us -
    it surrounds us everyday.
The ground before us crumbles,
    will we ever find our way?

Yet that unknown within us,
    is a force of great strength and might.
And if we press forward,
    the unknown within us will be seen in new light.

Fear Not

Fear not my little ones,
   whose feet have gone astray.
Whose misdirections and wanderings
   have increased with each new day.

Fear not, my child,
   who runs and hides his head.
Who slips and falls
   and at times has been misled -

to travel down broken roads
to stay with strangers
who eagerly lurk
in the shadows of sorrow and pain.

Do not feel condemned, cursed, or shamed -
   I'll always love you still the same.
Fear not my child,
   call out my name.

Beguiled and Betrayed

Beguiled and Betrayed
became friends one terrible day.
    Two lost souls, each half - now whole,
    confused, misguided, and out of control.

Never let Beguile betray you.
    He befriends the beleaguered band
of victims who have been conquered once again.
    He feels at home when you take his hand.

Beguiled and Betrayed
    want to become friends with you today.
Don't lose yourself, don't wander or stray -
    they hope to destroy your perfect new day.

Never let Beguile betray your soul.
He wants to see you lose control.
    To be beguiled or to be betrayed
    is to, all at once, become delayed -

from living the life you long to lead,
from giving good gifts to those in need.

Beguiled and Betrayed
became outcasts to me today.
And now my soul, at last, is whole,
I am complete and in control.

Your Life Has Just Begun

Point out the path you long to walk.
Listen to friends who need to talk.
Do what you know must be done.
Remember, your life has just begun.

Go About Doing Good!

Go about doing good
each and every day.
Stop and help a friend you know
who needs your help today.

Everyone needs a helping hand
to help them on their way,
so be the friend who helps someone
and start helping him today.

A Poet's Perception

A poet personifies perplexity.
He wanders o'er hill and vale.
He devours each day
as if famished for feelings,
but it won't help him decide what to say.

Distant lands and spiritual realms
continually keep him at bay.
The poet searches for answers and truth
but is dismissed and sent on his way.
He has no direction, no purpose, or plan,
but is searching for his voice and what he will say.

Ages roll foward and time ticks away,
truth is dispelled and replaced each day.
But the poet's voice rings out loud and clear
and we feel his presence ever near.

The poet personifies purity
and preaches of principles lost.
He examines the endeavors
of each woman and man,
and understands how much our perceptions cost.

Discipline Demanded a Demonstration

Discipline demanded a demonstration.
    Knowledge acknowledged the unknown.
Strength superceded its stamina,
    so the man walked on alone.

His shoulders supported the weight
    of the world's ever worrisome woes.
He carried within his calm, gentle trim,
    the hopes and fears of his foes.

Intelligence interrogated indolence.
    Integrity identified its ideal.
Benevolence bequeathed a beautiful blessing,
    and righteousness rewarded what is real.

Lost at Sea

I was lost at sea.
A sorry sailor
who was sinking fast,
surrounded by waves
and the fears of my past.

I had been shipwrecked
and abandoned.
I had been left to die
and was on my own.

I let out a cry -
at first, only faint.
But soon I was screaming
like mad.

I was actually lost at sea
surrounded by stillness -
isolation now
accompanied me.

Was this my end?
Was I destined to die?
Had the depths and abyss
heard my cry?

I was once lost at sea -
a sinking sailor
forced to pray
asking the heavens
to hear and obey.

I did not sink
or die that day.
God heard my prayer
and sent help my way.

Life is a Series of Decisions

Tell me, what have you learned?
Life is a series of lessons.
We are continually being taught each day.
Life is a series of decisions.
We all hope we will find our way.

Eternal Treasures

The knowledge you seek,
and the treasures you'll find,
are locked and stored
in the human mind.

Open your eyes,
see clearly my son.
The blessings of eternity
can someday be won.

Heart and soul,
body and mind -
freedom to seek
the blessings you'll find.

Begin today and earnestly seek
the treasures you hope you will find.
For eternal treasures are gifts from God
He lovingly offers to all mankind.

I Have But One Life to Live

I have but one life to live,
to serve and help and teach and give.
I have but one pure goal in life,
to comfort and ease the soul in strife.

Make Peace With Your Past

Please make peace with your past.
It comes and goes so fast.
Put the problems of your past behind you.
If you don't, your present can't last.

The Purifying Power of Patience

"I most eagerly await the day
　　when no problems come my way,"
was the sentence the young man uttered,
　　when he refused to kneel and pray.

"Why would God give us grief,
　　and struggle, and strife, and sin?
Why would He place us here on this earth,
　　with no possible hope to win?"

The father of the young man sat
　　in silence and hung his head.
He listened as his son bemoaned,
　　the life he'd learned to dread.

"My boy," the father meekly began,
"Grief is good. So is struggle and strife,
　　and truthfully, so is sin.
They all help us know we're not a lost cause -
　　especially when we fail and never win.

"Through struggle we find our hidden strength,
　　through strife we see the injustice of life.
These help us find perspective through pain
　　even with our grief and struggle and strife.

"There is a power that purifies
a power God grants unto man.
The ability to change one's circumstance,
if only we believe that we can."

The World is Yours...

The world is yours for the taking.
All that is good is yours for the keeping.
Good decisions are yours for the making.
Life's mysteries are yours for the seeking.

Search for truth, seek the right.
Follow goodness, embrace the light.

If you do all that you know you can do,
and if your decisions are pure and good -
then you will be great and accomplish so much,
now do all that you hope you would.

The World Does Not Revolve Around You

The world does not revolve around you.
You are not the star on the stage.
Know you are not the center of attention,
you are not the talk of the town.

Life has been lived before you were born
    and will continue to go on once more.
There are many acts that follow you,
    life will continue as it did before.

Do not be consumed by your constant talk,
    your chatter of self worth and import.
The world does not revolve around you,
    or any other selfish sort.

A Sunburn on My Soul

The other day,
   I got a sunburn on my soul.
A terrible and painful thing,
   but if I don't act fast it'll get out of control.

Someone was unkind to me,
   then another made me feel insecure -
at least that's what I tell myself
   I'm not entirely sure.

I felt betrayed, somehow,
   misguided, confused, and alone.
I feel others are judging me,
   I don't feel at all at home.

This sunburn scares me,
   for I think about how much worse it might be -
if I let these feelings go unchecked.
   You see, I feel imprisoned and long to be free.

The other day someone was kind to me,
   then another made me feel secure.
And that is what I've seen for myself,
   I know I'm entirely sure.

Sally Forth!

Sally Forth!
You've been summoned, my son.
The gods of greatness have called.
Hurry now, be steadfast, my son,
let apathy now be apalled.

Never let laziness linger.
Want is the wretch of the world.
Do not worship the idols of idleness.
Let hatred, from you, not be hurled.

So Sally Forth!
You have been summoned, my son.
The gods of greatness have called you.

Do not delay,
do not waste any time.
This day is yours,
it is truly sublime!

Friendship

I have been bound,
shackled and shorn,
tossed by the tempests of time -
carried about by changes unknown
and left to fend off these fiends on my own.

My time has brought me trials,
yet my trials have tempered my soul.
I've learned and changed and discovered new truths.
I've been empty, replenished, and completely made whole.

At times, emptiness has overtaken me.
I've been imprisoned on the Island of Isolation.
I've roamed with the ravages that ravaged my home,
I've been lost and alone and out of control.

But I have also been found.
I've been succored and saved,
tutored by the teachers of all time -
carried about by changes I've known
and embraced the good friends who remind me
I'm not alone.

Written in the Wind

The wishes that I wistfully wished
were written in the wind.
They were blown about and soon disappeared
and never came back again.

The thoughts I have thoughtlessly said,
without even thinking things through -
never amounted to much, never became anything
and the words that I wasted are deafening.

It is written in the the wind.
I wish that I could wistfully wish,
and be blown about and disappear -
and never return again.

But wishes that we wistfully wish
without even writing them down,
are wishes that can never amount to much -
and many a smile becomes a sad frown.

Never write your wishes in the wind,
unless you ask the wind to carry them
to those who need them most.

Help those around you and make wishes come true -
You'll feel better at once and enjoy life if you do.

Plan to Be Productive

I scan the surrounding vistas,
and span the open land.
I plan to be productive
and seek first to understand.

I'm searching for new answers
to questions I have not asked.
But there is work to be done
and tasks that must be tasked.

I can be productive.
I can produce positive results if I choose.
I can plan for success and grow and improve,
I will decide if I win or I lose.

Today I will be productive in my planning.
I will think about the good I can do.
And if there are struggles and problems arise,
I will work out a plan and do the best I can do.

The Thinker, The Speaker, and The Dreamer

The Thinker, thought he'd think a bit,
so The Speaker said he'd speak on it.
The Dreamer dreamt as dreamers do,
but The Persistent Doer just followed through.

Let me ask you -
Do we think about things?,
or even speak and daydream of things?
Do we make plans and talk it out
but never so much as work it out?

Yes, it is important, to think, and speak, and dream -
It's imperative to reflect and ponder and scheme.
But all our plans are of little or no worth
if we don't do that for which we were placed here on earth.

What is your purpose? What is your mission and calling?
What were you placed here to do?
Are you a thinker? A Speaker? Or possibly a Dreamer?
Or will you persist and just follow through?

Luck Lend a Hand

"Luck lend me a hand,"
is a phrase people shout -
when they don't want to work
but they hope everything will magically work out.

There are reasonably a fortunate few,
who have been blessed beyond their wildest dreams.
But most of these soon lose everything,
and luck, as we know, is not all that it seems.

But, rest assured, luck will lend you a hand
as you work as hard and as long as you can.

Luck lent me a hand
when I was prepared and had worked out a plan.
I gave it my all and did my best,
and in the end was prepared for luck's test.

The Stop Sign

A stop sign appeared out of the blue,
    and prevented me from moving on.
It signaled to me an emergency,
    and I knew that my good times were gone.

I traveled down the road with despair
    and knew that danger lurked everywhere.
I was too cautious and careful and did not live,
    and soon I stopped going anywhere.

All I saw were stop signs -
    they appeared everywhere I went.
And every day and night I soon grew tired
    and my energy was always spent.

I feared I'd see more stop signs,
    for they popped up around me each day.
And wherever I went and whatever I did
    I was afraid I'd turn myself away.

But I will not allow unnecessary stop signs
    to deter me with each new day.
I will create my own road map,
    for now I have found my way.

Stature and Strength

You came here to meet a champion today,
    a man of great stature and strength.
But instead you meet this fraud of a man,
    and you soon will know why at length.

At times I pretend to be more than I actually am,
because it helps me face my fears and stand.
    And force a smile and try to be
    something more than you actually see.

I've claimed many victories
    as if I were a mighty man.
But truth be told, I'm not at all,
    and at times I need a helping hand.

Every champion has fallen before.
    Each has been battered and bruised.
And most find new strength when they've fallen,
    but many feel beaten and abused.

We can all be champions together -
    each of us has spiritual stature and strength.
And one day you will meet your own true self,
    and will discover who you are at length.

Finding a Need

I am a prisoner of my past.
My choices have placed me where I am now,
but these chains I have made for myself are not mine.
I will set myself free and recapture my time.

I go where I am prompted to go -
where the whispering wind leads and guides me.
I go where I'm needed, where I can serve and give.
I go to set other fellow prisoners free.

Every day I see my fellow inmates who need my help.
We all are imprisoned by the deeds we do
each of us needs guidance and wisdom and love,
and we all need help from God above.

The Stranger Who Smiled

I shared a smile with a stranger
who looked as though he needed one.
He looked so sad and seemed so low
so I nodded and smiled and said hello.

The stranger looked up and smiled at me.
He chuckled and waved and came toward me.
He then hugged me and thanked me for what I had done.
And told me my smile had been the only one.

No one had smiled at the stranger or said hello.
The stranger had been there most of the day,
but every other person had gone with the flow
and no one had smiled or walked his way.

As we said our goodbyes the stranger smiled again
and told me that God would bless me today.
He told me that God would answer my prayer
and angels would help me and love would be there.

I shared a smile with a stranger
who must have known that I needed his care.
He must have seen how my spirit was weak
and so God whispered to him, "Help that man over there."

The Rain is Falling Down

The rain is falling down.
    It's dancing on the ground.
It tiptoes on the tulips
    and saturates the sound...

of silence, and loneliness,
    of emptiness, and pain -
of heartache and unhappiness
    and sorrow and shame.

The rain is a purifying power
    it cleanses the barren land.
It tries to heal the sorrow earth feels
    and waits for mankind to rise and stand.

One Voice Becomes Two

There are so many voices
that chatter and clammer and fuss.
They make a big deal -
some scream and yell and some might even cuss.

These voices outnumber
our solitary sound.
When we speak on our own
we fall flat on the ground.

But one voice becomes two,
and then two become four,
and before you know it
we become more and more.

You Do Not Hear Me...

You see me, but you do not hear me.
I hear you but we never see eye to eye.
Our inability to communicate and connect
is a terrible plight -
a confounding connundrum -
more than just a mere oversight.

It is a misunderstanding between wrong and right -
an inability to comprehend and see the light.

You hear me, but you do not see me.
Will we ever see eye to eye?
Our lack of communication creates a disconnect
between our hearts and souls.

Please see me, and hear me with your heart.
Listen to all I say be aware of all I do.
All I hope to achieve in life,
is to be loved and admired by you.

Conquer Thyself

Self conquest is a noble quest -
an adventurous journey to take.
But most live life as if they were the guest
and their selfish pursuits make them seem quite fake.

Faith moves us forward
while fear moves us back.
Light continually illuminates us
while darkness perpetually blinds us.

Conquer thyself and
"To thine own self be true!"
but be true to the goodness
in others too.

Self conquest cannot consume one's self.
It should not overshadow one's will to live.
Be true to the best that is within yourself,
and think of what you, to life, can give.

I Choose...

I am the one to decide and choose
    what future fate I'll befriend.
What positive characteristics I'd like to possess
    and who I hope I'll become in the end.

I choose to be happy.
I choose to be true.
    I choose to be honest and good.
I choose to help others and believe in the best.
    I choose to do what I should.

I choose not to listen
    as the naysayers cluck -
complaining about misfortunes
    and their aversion to luck.

If I can decide and choose for myself
    then I possess powers beyond belief.
I can assist and I can endeavor
    to provide others with necessary relief.

I choose to be noble.
I choose to be brave.
    I choose to believe I can.
I choose to improve and outdo myself -
    I choose to be better than I currently am.

I Have Strength and Courage Once More

I speak as one speaks,
   who knows not what to say.
Whose deliberate attempts to do one's best
   has discouraged him day after day.

My silent voice does not speak with strength.
   My timid soul hides in corners and fears
what future foibles I may endure -
   what unnecessary heartache will bring me tears.

Where is my voice?
Why can't I speak and stand up for truth
instead of being so weak?

My once silent voice has now found its voice.
   I have strength and courage once more.
I can stand atop any mountaintop
   or freely walk upon any ocean shore.

The Improved Version of a Better Me

The man I was and the man I am,
will become the man I long to be.
The improved version of a better me
is the man I long to see.

But I am that man
and I always have been.
I didn't know it,
but now I do and I must be true.

You see my past, present, and future,
are eternally present for me.
I am my past, I cannot forget it -
even though there are moments I often regret it.

And presently I battle
with the man I currently am
because I remember who I once was
but I now know I'll be who I already am.

I look forward to the future for I see myself -
the me I know I will one day be.
And the man I already know I eternally am.
At last, I have set my true self free.

Worry and Guilt

Worry and guilt are the best of friends
in the worst imaginable way.
Guilt reminds worry that everything is wrong.
And worry frets about it all day long.

The more worry frets the more nervous guilt becomes.

So worry and guilt stay side by side -
loyal through thick and thin.
Don't ever let these two attach themselves to you!
They will destroy you in the end.

I Am More...

I am more than merely what meets the eye,
what people think when they pass by.
  I am more than what my failure shows,
    there is so much more that no one knows.

I am more than my weakness,
  and more than my fear,
I am more than my loneliness,
  and what others can't hear.

I am more than a shadow
  or thought or a sign,
I am more than a stranger,
  or traveler through time.

I am more than even what I can see,
there is so much more I long to be.
  I am more than my thoughts, my feelings or heart,
  I have more I must learn and more to impart.

I am more it is true, but others have learned much more
  than I, but I can learn and follow and try.
We are more than we think - you and I,
  and we can accomplish whatever we try.

Motivate Me!

Motivate me!
Not by what you say,
for the world is full of speakers like you,
who can talk and talk until their face turns blue.

In the quiet moments
after the crowds have gone away -
when the world has forgotten you
and even turned away from you -
that is when I hope you'll be true,
and will continue to do
what you motivate others to do.

So motivate me!
Not just by what you say,
but by what you continue to do
when the world completely ignores you.

Hidden Hazards

There are hidden hazards all around
    they surround us every day.
Heinously horrible hazards lurk -
    in every step along the way.

One misstep may destroy us!
    One wrong turn takes away
every worthwhile step we have taken,
    in our past and earlier day.

These hidden hazards hurt us.
    They hinder our progress and impede.
Though hindsight identifies these adversaries as such -
    they want us to believe we will never succeed.

Do not let hidden hazards harm you.
There is nothing pretty about pernicious problems.
    They poisen and pollute,
    they debilitate and dillute.

Hidden hazards harrass us,
    they harm us in every way.
So, do not harbour hidden hazards -
    quickly run away.

The State of Sadness

The sorry state of sadness
that saturates the soul -
that sprinkles sickness and then spreads sorrow
and subdues us to feeling alone...

is unthinkable!
It makes us be unreasonable.
It's entirely unfathomable,
and completely unimaginable.

I'm sorry to say that the state of sadness
completely sickens my soul.
It encourages unhappiness where happiness should dwell,
It makes complete men feel inadequate.
It's a frightening and terrible blow.

Sadness starts out small
and then grows in an unruly way.
It soon overtakes its suspects,
and destroys them day by day.

Life is full of thorns and roses,
the good and the bad abound.
But if we neglect the beauty beside us,
no good will ever be found.

The Force of Habit

The force of habit is good and bad,
    its strength is uncommonly strong.
It can help us do whatever we choose,
    we're empowered to pursue right or wrong.

This force of habit reclaims young and old,
    it does not discriminate at all.
The habits that befall us are the ones we choose,
    we have no one to blame if we fall.

A good habit can produce a better you -
a more productive and effective soul.
But our habits are a reflection of the thoughts we think.
So ultimately, we should know we are the ones in control.
Take control of your life by the habits you form.
The daily decisions you make in turn
    will teach you and define you,
    they will perfect you and eventually refine you.

This force of habit is a powerful friend,
    an ally to be championed and sought.
And as your habits, in turn, refine you,
    the battles you face will be fought.

Intrinsic Intelligence

I met a man whose name was might
   and his strength was great and he was bold.
I met another whose name was truth,
   and he was honest, good, and old.

Might was young and fearless and did
what few of his own ever dreamed they could.
    Truth, though old, was in fact, very bold.
    He was steadfast, and honest, a sight to behold.

I asked myself what I could give...
what I could be or do or share.
    For I do not have great strength or might,
    and I would not be one to bring truth to light.

But I can think for myself -
   and project and plan.
I may not be the strongest or wisest of men,
   but I can prepare like any man.

I can prepare for the good and the bad.
I can set my course and follow my plan.
    I can do my best and improve each day,
    and be the best in my own little way.

Teach Me

You are smart.
You are brave.
You can teach.
You can save.
You are kind.
You are true.
You are powerful.
You are you.

Dreamers in the Clouds

Around the world, in ships I sail,
amid the castles in the sky.
And touch the Heavens and the veil,
of future dreams that I pass by.

The world about me revolves, in turn,
as dreamers explore new worlds anew.
And I continue my search once more
and discover which dreams are worth fighting for.

You Will Not Destroy Me!

Be gone!
Bewailing and bewitching bereavement.
Beleaguer me no more.

Be away with you!
Be done with me.
I have more strength in store.

You cannot upset me.
You will not destroy me.
I choose to live life and be free.
You will not stop me,
from doing my best...
I've learned how to hope and believe.

You will not upset me.
You cannot destroy me.
I will live my life and be free!

So BE GONE!
Bewailing and bewitching bereavement.
You've served your purpose - now let me be.

To Rest and to Play

I look at my mirror of life, and say,
"What good will come my way?"
For my trials and woes seem too much today,
and I long for some freedom to rest and play.

To rest from my worries and calm my fears,
to drink in my dreams and brush away these tears.

That mirror of my life reflects what I see,
but that reflection is my perception and it also hinders me.

I broke my mirror that reflected my strife
and instead I'm looking for a hope filled life.
I will help others with trials and woes today,
and help them find freedom to rest and play.

Choice of Volition

Choose and decide!
The power to determine your future is yours.
Do not run and hide!

Your choice is your volition.
Your determinent mind
is your key to ambition.

The choices of life
can ensnare or ennoble,
empower or tear down at will.

It matters not what trials may come...
    each must face their fears some day.
But what we do in those sacred seconds
    describe to us what our hearts truly say.

The choice of a lifetime is given today.
    We choose the path we wish to pursue.
It does not follow us, we always summon it...
    which is why it must forever be true.

Choose and decide!
The power to determine your future is yours.
You cannot run and hide!

Perfection is Imperfect

Perfection is imperfect...
in its imperfectly perfect way.
It creates the ideal
that is anything but ideal
to help us perfect our imperfect day.

Perfection sets the standard
for the imperfect to hopefully obtain.
But perfection continually eludes us -
so imperfection becomes the refrain.

We are perfectly imperfect.
But we should not seek imperfection.

There should be a complete rejection
of our own imperfection.
There must be a reconnection
to the pursuit of progressing toward true perfection.

Let us perfect our own imperfections,
though we continue to be perfectly imperfect.
We will now direct our attention
to our best intention of our future imperfect perfection.

When Wrongs Have Been Righted

When wrongs have been righted
    the light reappears,
and smiles return
    in the absence of tears.

When hearts have been broken
    and one's trust disappears...
the darkness of doubt
    awakens our fears.

Right and wrong have warred before
    in every time and season past.
But each new wrong re-opens the wound
    and the rightness of truth is fading fast.

So we must right the wrongs we do
and always be faithful and honest and true.

When wrongs can be righted
    the light will re-appear...
and everyone, in turn, will smile
    to know that truth will always be near.

Don't You Quit!

Don't you quit!
I'll hear none of it!
Do your best and continue forward.
    Face your fears and move along...
    and you'll find that problems help you be strong.

Problems pave your future path.
    They prepare you for what you'll face.
They prepare you for who you are destined to be...
    if you quit, you will encounter disgrace.

But don't be discouraged or disheartened at all,
    Shift with the sands of time.
Never give up on yourself, my boy,
    even when you've spent your last nickel or dime.

Walk with courage and stand with strength.
    And all the good you seek will come.
Never quit, my beloved son,
    the victory over life comes to everyone.

Let Go of Perfection

You don't have to be
first in line,
or have all of the right answers,
all of the time.

Let go of perfection.
It doesn't need you
and you don't need it.

Stand on your own.
Let imperfection take hold.
Welcome it. Embrace it. You're not alone!

Please Show Kindness to Everyone

Please show kindness to everyone.
Everyone needs our love.
Every person must hear sweet words divine,
each voice must be strengthened - both yours and mine.

Some are prone to worry.
That's nothing you don't know...
but far too many live life in a hurry,
and many adults are not encouraged to grow.

So please show kindness to everyone.
For everyone needs our love.
Every person must speak sweet words divine,
each voice must be heard - both yours and mine.

The Eloquence of Your Example

The eloquence of your example
   is something that poets preach.
It's finesse is truly fantastic...
   yet somehow, it seems, a bit out of reach.

Heros hearken and hear my hopeful words.
What you say means nothing
   if you defile it by what you do.
For your words are truly worthless
if your actions deny what your words imply...
   for you must do more than you say you will do.

The eloquence of your example
can be heard by what others have seen you do.
You cannot sacrifice your stature, my friend,
   or seek to live a lie underneath.
You cannot cover up a thousands sins
   or boast of the brilliance of your bloodstained sheath.

Everyone has a disheartening past
   filled with mistakes and regret.
But live today before it slips away...
   the past has been lived so we will never forget.

Divine Design

It is, in fact, divine design
when two opposing ideas align.
    When friend and foe come face to face
    and when neither one leaves in disgrace.

You see, my friend, divine design
    is destined to set you free.
It's a higher law - a better way
    it helps you be who you were born to be.

There is, in truth, divine within,
    every single woman and man.
The greatness of God - the glories of man,
    they compell us to follow God's purer plan.

It is, in truth, divine design...
when opposing parties at last align.
    When foe and friend, at last, embrace,
    and when both of these have found their place.

Each Life is a Majestic Masterpiece

Help and lift those who fall.
Comfort and cradle those who cry.
Encourage and motivate those who stall,
weep for and revere those who die.

Each life is a majestic masterpiece...
celebrate each soul's celestial symphony.
Can you hear the heavens sing?
Lift your praise and let it ring.

The Evidence of Greatness

"I have been given the strength of lions," he said,
and as a coward he roared to the crowd.
"I have amassed my fortune throughout foreign lands,"
and then he smiled as each head meekly bowed.

We see this scene unfold night and day
as men fight for fortune and fame.
A callous caravan of cowards all around...
names change, but their lives are the same.

The evidence of greatness is not a shallow thing.
It's not a frivolous fancy or even a flippant thing.

You see, greatness needs no evidence
to justify its worth.
It needs no shouts of self-import
for we are born with greatness at birth.

I Hear the Bells

I hear the bells
that sweetly chime
of blessings past
and love divine.

I see the scenes
of heavenly dreams
of noble hopes
and upset schemes.

I taste the nectar
of sweetness divine
and hear the bells
that lovingly chime.

The Gates of Greatness

Meet me at the gates of greatness
  where the greatest minds convene.
Where simplicity's sublime invitation
  will uncover mysteries the world has never seen.

At the gates of greatness...
the wise invite the willing.
  The eager souls who want to know...
  the humble heros who yearn to grow.

You were born with gifts of greatness.
  Your birthright is marvelous and pure.
You will change the course of history,
  you will be good and noble for sure.

The gates of greatness beckon you...
  only you can answer their call.
They'll open their gates and welcome you,
  their invitation is given to all.

Please, Bring Me Light

Bring me light
when I sit in darkness.
　　Even when I tell you to go away,
don't listen to me, and please forgive me.
　　But you must help me find my way.

Bring me light
when I shut out the world around me.
When I pretend I don't care
and believe no one's there.
　　Don't listen to a word I say.
Help me forgive myself
　　and show me a better way.

Bring me light
when I feel as if all is lost,
and I fear my trials are a terrible cost.
Don't listen to what I tell you -
　　and do not turn me away.
I need your help and I need your prayers,
　　please help me find my way!

The Maze of Mediocrity

In shadows I sit and sulk,
in corners I cower in fear.
I've made a maze that maddens me...
my own personal maze of mediocrity.

I've done this to myself each day
time and time again.
I sing this familiar and well sung refrain
and yet this song bears my name.

A maze of mediocrity
which way do I go each day?
My maze of mediocrity -
I cannot find my way.

I've lost myself
and don't know how to find me.
I hope and think I know myself
but lately I cannot clearly see.

What is this maze that surrounds me?
My own personal maze of mediocrity.

And yet, I am not mediocre at all,
no one truly is.

We each hold divinity within our souls,
each is a master in the making.
Life is given to those who keep giving...
and depleted from those who never stop taking.

Right and Wrong

Right met wrong as they traveled along.
Right spoke of truth but wrong only spoke
of what didn't belong.
Right paved the path of the good and the just.
Wrong created the way of lies and lust.

We travel with right and wrong each day,
but only we can choose our way.

Hum-il-ity

Hum-il-ity is a humble little tune
they hum in the quaint town of Humbville
    where folks don't pretend to be what they're not
and everyone is closed-lipped
    about the blessings they've got.

Every conversation focuses on them - not you.
Every intention focuses on the many - not the few.
    It's not about sharin' everything you know.
It's more about seein' others shine
    (you don't need the glow).

Hum-il-ity is a nice little diddy
    these great souls teach their children to sing.
The proud are few and the meek are many
and even though they know so much...
    they don't feel the need to share everything!

Hum-il-ity, Hum-il-ity - a humble little tune.
The meek can sing...the proud cannot
the weak can learn...the loud shall not.

Hum-il-ity, Hum-il-ity - sing this humble song.
Hum-il-ity, Hum-il-ity - hum it all day long!

The Beaten Man

I felt at once like a beaten man
who had lost his will to live.
  A sorry silhouette of a shadow of pain...
  a man who lost everything and had nothing to gain.

I've looked back on myself at those terrible times
and prayed I'd look forward to a better day.
  When light would return and hope would abound...
  and my new self, and old self, would at last be found.

I feel right now like a changed man,
  who has learned from the mistakes of my past.
I see more clearly because I feel more deeply...
  and that beaten man is fading fast.

Every man and woman feels beaten and broken at times.
  We've all lost our way many times before -
and yet, in life, we are given new days...
  more blessings are always in store.

Decide What You'll Do

Smile and let sunshine surround you.
Frown and the world falls down around you.
When you smile or frown others see you.
But only you can decide what you'll do.

Succeed and Know

Be. Do.
Learn and grow.
Begin. Attempt.
Succeed and know.

The Mirror of Meaning

I stammered and struggled
I sulked and cried,
when the world would not go my way.
I looked at myself and felt betrayed,
when I couldn't change my night to day.

Everything seemed meaningless,
for nothing was as it seemed.
And everything had turned out painfully wrong,
and wasn't at all what I'd dreamed.

I looked at myself in the mirror that night
and wondered who I was.
Where was the hopeful and dream driven man
who had challenged me to face each new day?

Was he hiding? Was he missing?
Had my doubts and fears shamed him away?

I murmured and muddled like a man left alone
to face the cold world - entirely on his own.

The mirror of meaning is meaningless -
it does not mean a thing...
unless the face is listening
to their reflection of hope and a dream.

A Light on the Path Before You

There is a light on the path before you.
　　There is hope in your future days.
There is a promise of peace in store for you...
　　the sun shines upon you its heavenly rays.

Soak up sunshine wherever you go.
　　Look to the light and learn to live.
Find the beauty in every soul -
　　ask what, to them, you can give.

Everyone has a talent within...
　　a good only they can give.
Find the goodness within each one
　　and, though dying, you'll start to live.

The World is at Your Feet

Look at the world around you.
    There are so many people to meet.
Become a life traveler and experience it all...
    the world is at your feet.

Face the World

Do not be afraid to face the world.
    Rise up and live life today.
Do not be ashamed of your place in the world...
    If you know who you are you will find your way.

Loving Faith

It takes sturdy hands to build a home
of concrete, brick, and stone...
and tender hands to warm the heart
of one who feels alone.

We all must help the ones we love
and teach them faith in God above.
Give unselfish service to those so dear
and loving faith to calm their fear.

The Sweet Refrain

I'm glad to be alive.
Glad to be living through the storm.
I'll endure my trials and will not mourn.

Life to me is filled with luster...
with beauty and strength and happiness.
It's the sweet refrain of all I hope to gain.
It's peace and excitement and goodness.

I'm glad to be learning
by embracing education and truth.
I'm glad to be working,
glad to be earning,
glad to be teaching
and mentoring our youth.

The Opportunity to Do Something Good

I don't think of it as an obligation or a duty.
but rather, as an opportunity
to serve, uplift, and edify...
to teach, instruct, and glorify -
to do the good that oft I should.

The opportunity to do something good
    for the benefit of all around
is an opportunity I long to have -
    an investment that is entirely sound.

Potential and Power and Truth

There's greatness within each tiny seed,
    there is a palace within each brick.
There is speed and swiftness within each steed,
    and a brilliant light within each wick.

There is wisdom within the foolish mistakes
    each individual commits each day.
Each step forward we take, in turn,
    will help us find our way.

There is greatness within you.
    There is potential and power and truth.
You have intelligence and understanding...
    even though some might mock your youth.

You will find the greatness within each seed.
You will build your palace brick by brick.

There is greatness within you.
    You are potential and power and truth.
You have intelligence and understanding...
    no one will ever question the intent of your youth.

The Currents of Change

Do not confine yourself to constant chastisement,
flow with the currents of change.
Do not surround yourself with conniving creatures...
those who are stubborn and remain the same.
Change is a powerful ally -
a cause to be championed and won.
Do not fear change - it continues to come,
but all who embrace it have already won.

The Endless Pit of Despair

The endless pit of despair is deep and wide
and far too many fall inside.
They don't always intend to, but sometimes they do
because it's where they try and hide
from responsibility and the world
and the good they could do,
and the fears of the many
and the dreams of a few
that frighten and astonish them
and often puzzle them too.

If you have ever felt despair before,
please know you are not alone.
Others have been there and know your pain.
With love there is strength and hope to gain.

Do Your Best at Whatever You Do!

The determined man will see it through...
the tasks he's been asked to perform or do.
He's committed to improving and doing his best -
undaunted by each challenge of each daily test.

Ambitious and focused is the woman with a dream,
who's not afraid to work and lead her team
to victory and success, to triumph and reward -
she rarely has time to be lazy or bored.

"Rome was not built in a day," they say,
so the successful individual continues day by day
working and refining when most men quit,
but the successful individual wants none of it.

So, see it through and do your best at whatever you do.
Be committed to improve and you'll pass each test.
And each day you'll know
you will be your best.

How Do You Do?

How do you do?
It's a wonder to see you out here.
Does the air chill you?
Do you feel frightened and alone and afraid?
You've separated yourself
from the masses and the many
and you now set foot on a glorious road
where few have dared to walk.

The path before you is an adventurous one
with excitement of the new and the unknown.
You are destined to do great things, my friend...
know you are not alone!

Decide What You Want

When you get up in the morning...
have a pep talk with yourself.
Give yourself an agenda and discuss what you'll do.
Decide what you'll accomplish and where you
need to improve.

Don't leave life up to fate...
wishing that things will turn out great.
Examine your life - decide what you'll do...
there are opportunities and possibilities for you.

If you aren't happy and you're not content,
don't get angry, swear, or vent.
Develop a plan and see it through.
Decide what you want and what you'll need to do.

A Wonderful Word!

Mother is a wonderful word,
we speak most reverently.
Mother, we thank you
for all that you are,
and all that you
help us to be!

You Cannot Capture Creativity

You cannot capture creativity,
you cannot force it to do what you will.
Its power surrounds you,
and then impales you,
and illuminates your mind
to the treasures it finds.

Indecisive and Incapable

Indecisive and Incapable
are sinister siblings at best.
One dreads a decision -
and the other abstains from ability.
And both will eventually fail life's test.

Activate Your Potential

Activate your potential,
   your possibilities are profound.
Activate your potential,
   infinite options always abound.
You are more than your past.
   Your future is glorious and great!
Trust in all that you will someday do -
   don't leave your life up to fate!

The Pats on the Back I Give Myself

The pats on the back that I give myself
　　and the cheers I laud in self-praise,
do nothing to help me help others beside me
　　it's a waste of my minutes, my hours, and days.

Everytime I coddle my broken heart
　　or tell myself I am the best,
I bring out the worst within myself,
　　and eventually I fail life's test.

Instead, I will find, other backs to pat,
　　and let them know that they are the best.
I will speak of their greatness and honor their name,
　　and eventually, I pray, I may pass life's test.

Time to Grow

There are many things I do not know.
  I have so much more to learn.
I'm like a tree that tries to grow -
  I'm always waiting my turn.

But time will come and time will go.
  Life always moves me along.
And while I go throughout my life,
  I'll sing a thankful song.

Light Illuminate My Way

Light illuminate my way
  through the valleys of viciousness and greed.
Over hills of harrassment and destruction,
  to a promised land that I desperately need.

Light was my constant companion
  even if I walked down a darkened street.
Light was there to give me hope
  and to steady my wandering feet.

Seeds of Self Destruction

Do not plant seeds of self destruction.
You'll always reap what you sow.

Do not persuade others down terrible paths,
that you know you would never go.

Be Determined

Be determined to do what's right.
To follow your conscience with all your might.

Be inspired to be a light.
That you may have strength for the battles you fight.

The Birth of a Child

The birth of a child
is sweet and pure
a beautiful experience
to witness and behold.
A spiritual sight I long to see
when new life is given
and the child is set free.

Be Your Best (in all you do)

Be the woman or man you long to be,
the goodness you hope others will one day see.
Be the arms that others embrace,
when met with hard times and overcome by disgrace.

Be the smile that spreads near and far.
Be the example wherever you are.
Be your best in all you do.
Be God's helper to those who need you.

Be a Little Better Today

Be a little more patient
   when problems perplex you today.
Be a little more forgiving,
   if others are unkind to you today.

If others speak hurtful or untrue words,
   do not retaliate or do the same.
Know you are better than what they say,
   think of your legacy and your good name.

Be a little better today
   than you have been before.
You'll be better off for it -
   think of the blessings that are in store.

Eternity

By deed and by thought
by word and by creed -
I etch in the heavens

IMMORTALITY.

By faith and by virtue
by repentance and by love -
I stretch to the heavens

AND TOUCH ETERNITY.

Try to Fly

Spread your wings and fly.
The time has come for you to soar.
You don't know what you
can accomplish in life
until you attempt and actively try.

The time has come for you
to spread your wings and fly.
Go on and see the world,
you won't know what you will accomplish
until you put yourself out there and try.

Spread Smiles

A smile is a frown,
    that's been turned upside down.
And a frown is a smile,
    that's tripped and fallen down.

If you chance to meet someone
who looks like their smile is about to fall down -
pick them up before they stumble,
and help them spread smiles all over your town.

Happy Helpers

Hearken and hear the happy helpers,
who heed the hero's call.
Those who see what needs abound
will behold the blessings they've already found.

Little Successes Move Me Along

Never again will I overlook
    the needful necessities that must be done.
The day to day duties I alone must do
    and the little obstacles I must overcome.

Little successes move me along.
They encourage me and strengthen me
until each day is done.

Little successes move me along.
    I am seeing small changes each day.
These little successes will help me be strong,
    I am growing in my own little way.

Be the Person You Want to Be

Don't get worked up, have a tissy fit, and cry
when things go wrong and you think you'll die.
From embarrassment and shame and ego and pride,
and you want to run and you try to hide.

Don't you fret and don't you frown
when the life you knew gets turned upside down.
When past mistakes pop up again.
When problems and deadlines occur now and then.

Don't live your life in a reckless way
in a fashionable façade where you play a part.
Simply be the person you know you should be,
and live the life you truly want to lead.

Be Genuine and Be Sincere

Be genuine and be sincere.
Do not mistrust and do not fear.
Listen to the unlearned.
Always befriend the friendless.
Be quick to forgive the tyrant,
but never be unruly or defiant.

Please be genuine and please be sincere.
If you trust you shall not fear.
Listen to others - love them for who they are,
and if you do, life will take you very far.

When Life Calls

When you fall - fall forward.
Face your future self.
When life calls - call to it,
and be at peace with your true self.

Listen, See, and Live

Listen with your heart.
See with your soul.
Live with your imagination,
that your life may be complete and whole.

What Will Life Say About You?

People are quite productive
and most are quite resourceful.
Most do their best
and most pass the test -

What will life say about you?

We are all quite unique,
with individual talents and traits all our own.
We each have our own little life to lead -

What will your life say about you?

When the Heavens Open

There are times, every now and again,
when the heavens open and truth is revealed.
Where courage is found and strength is gained.
Where the wrongs are made right and all that is good
is obtained.

Happiness Comes From the Heart

Happiness is not hidden
in a superficial fantasy land.
It is not an ideology
or a product you can hold in the palm of your hand.

Happiness comes from the heart.
It's the only place where true happiness can start!

Speak Softly

Speak softly when the stillness stirs.
When sad times and sorrows scream.
Gently whisper when the newness nears
when through the darkness a small light shall beam.

Listen as the silence speaks
hear its hallowed words.

Look Around

Look around as you lead the life you live.
Open your ears and hear your heart.
Listen to what it says!

The Preacher and the Sinner

The preacher and the sinner
sat down and had some dinner.
The preacher confessed he was no saint,
and the sinner explained that he
was sorry for an unbecoming past -
but knew that he might one day be
more saintly and noble and pure and free.

The preacher shared his shortcomings,
and the sinner intently listened.
Then the sinner counseled the preacher,
before they finished their dinner.

You see, the preacher and the sinner,
are one and two of the same.
Each of us is the preacher and sinner
and each of us can feel like a loser and winner.

The sinner, at times, does not want the preacher,
but the preacher always loves the sinner.
And by the grace of God and the goodness of man,
the Heavens are preparing our eternal dinner.

Get Up and Get Going

Get up and get going.
Once you begin you'll be on your way.
Never stop dreaming of where you will go.
Let your someday begin today!

Perspective

Keep an eye on what is coming.
See what is in store.
Set your sights on truly seeing
your perspective is better than it was before.

I Beseech Thee

I beseech thee
to bequeath all thy worldly goods
to the brotherhood of humanity,
to the shackled souls who are lost in the woods.

Subdue thy soul.
Heal thine heart and take control.
Freely give and selflessly serve -
that you, one day, may be perfectly whole.

Rally the Troops

Rally the troops
strike up the band.
Lead from the front
you're in command.

The troops will follow their leader.
They're waiting for you to stand.
Lead by example and do your best,
teach those you lead to command.

Knock on the Door

Knock on the door and ask for shelter
and sustenance and spirit and strength.
Sit on the floor and ask for wisdom,
and the determination to find it at length.

I Am a Conscious Creator

I am a conscious creator.
  I consciously create my day.
From start to finish...from morning to night
  I'll search and find my way.

I'll think about what I'm doing.
  I'll reflect upon what's been done.
I'll consciously decide to choose the best
  until, at last, life's victory is won.

A Better You

Start today and see it through.
  Work your way and do what you do.
Be your best and give it your all...
  and each day you'll become a better you.

Be

Be positive and proactive.
Be courageous but be kind.
Be intelligent and interactive,
as you seek you likewise shall find.

Don't Forget

Be peaceful. Be calm.
Do not say things you may regret.
Be cheerful...but be tender.
Remember these words, and don't forget.

Courage is Here

Never fear. Courage is here.
Do not fret, your goal has been set.
Do not worry, you are not in a hurry.
Please do not fear, courage is near.

Every Season of Life

In every season of life
there is something to be gained.
There are lessons we can learn,
and values to obtain.

I do not speak of riches,
    at least, not in a worldly way.
For eternal blessings are in store for us
    if we will walk God's chosen way.

How you treat another
    and what you do and say,
speaks loud volumes of who you are
    and who you try to become each day.

So in every season of your life,
    seek for something good you can gain.
Life lessons help us continue to learn,
    as we work on life's problems and push past our pain.

In every season of our life
there is always something new to be gained.
So teach life lessons and help others learn
the values they hope they'll obtain.

Be Not Afraid

Be not afraid
  to do all the good you can -
to serve, uplift, and edify
  every child, woman, or man.

Be not afraid
  to speak out when truth needs to hear your voice!
You can share logic and reason and hope.
  Choose the best in life - it's always your choice.

So BE NOT AFRAID.
  Simply do all the good you can -
and serve, uplift, and edify
  every child, woman, and man.

God's Counsel

Be slow to speak and quick to listen,
    was the counsel He asked me to heed -
but I interrupted His wise advice
    and told Him what I felt I might need.

Be swift to serve and quickly forgive
    was the advice He hoped I would learn.
But I was too busy helping myself
    and seeking the success I thought I should earn.

I had set God aside, thinking that I knew best.
But in life I began to fail each and every test.

Everything was somehow different now.
    I was lost and had forgotten God's truth.
He asked me to serve and to quickly forgive -
    but I had forsaken these lessons I learned in my youth.

So now I'm oh so slow to speak and very quick to listen.
    There is so much counsel God wants me to heed
I will not interrupt His wise advice -
    For God knows exactly what I need.

I will be swift to serve and quickly forgive,
there is so much I still must learn.
    I will busy myself with serving mankind
    and the success I seek is what God wants me to find.

Begin Again

Begin again whenever you must.
 Life is filled with despair and disdain
but the ones who adapt and continue to change
 are the ones who overcome their momentary pain.

Everyone falls and fails at times,
 but those who continue and work through grief
are the ones who inspire us and help us see
 that as we improve we increase our belief.

We believe in ourselves and humanity
 and all the good we can do with each day.
We believe we can help those around us improve
 and we all can progress as we find our own way.

Life is filled with happiness and hope,
 there is so much goodness around.
And as we serve others and sacrifice and give
 true happiness will always be found.

Another poetry book by **Jerald Simon**:

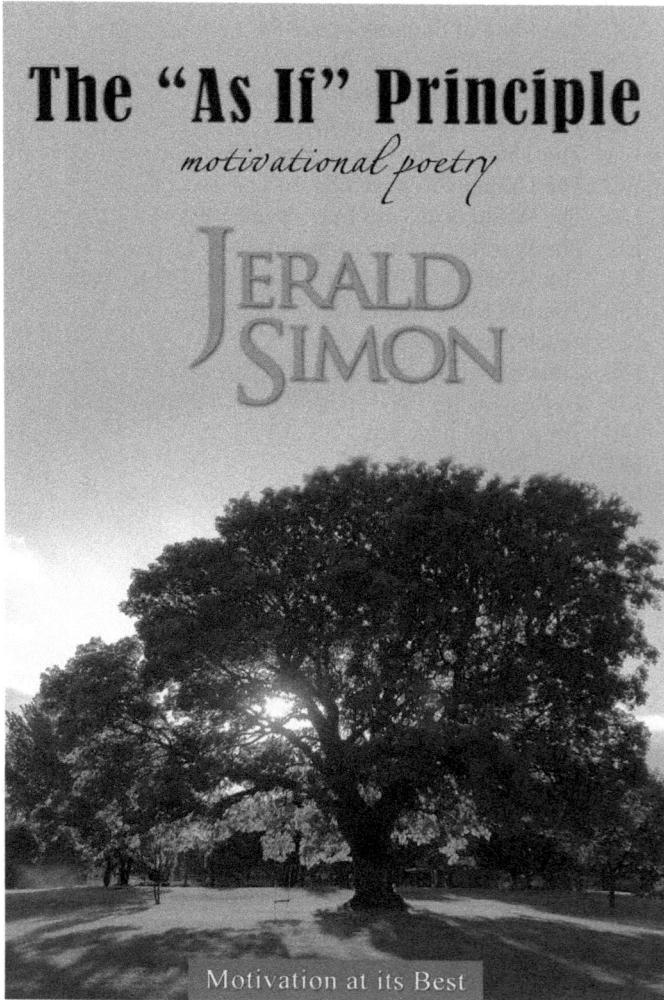

The "As If" Principle

motivational poetry

JERALD SIMON

Motivation at its Best

Available from Amazon and other Retailers

Other motivational and inspirational books by Jerald Simon...

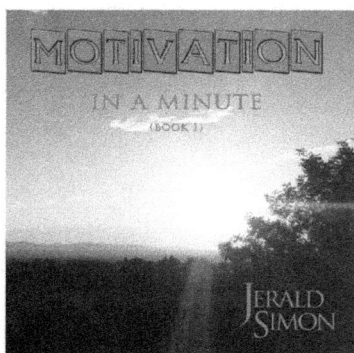

Motivation in a Minute and **Perceptions, Parables, and Pointers** by JERALD SIMON (read more at this link): **http://musicmotivation.com/ shop/motivationalself-help-books/perceptions-parables-and-pointers-by-jerald-simon/**

The main goal in writing down these perceptions, parables, and pointers, and in creating this book in general, is to present ideas that will help get people thinking, imagining, planning, creating, and actively participating in life.

The "As If" Principle (motivational poetry) by JERALD SIMON features 222 original motivational poems written by Simon to inspire and motivate men, women, businesses, organizations, leaders, mentors, advisers, teachers, and students. The poems were written to teach values and encourage everyone everywhere to do and be their best. (read more at this link): **http://musicmotivation.com/shop/motivationalself-help-books/the-as-if-principle-by-jerald-simon/**

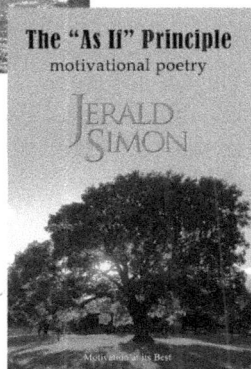

I have several CDs of original music I have composed that I would love to have you listen to. You can listen to my music on Spotify, Pandora, etc., or purchase my music on iTunes, Amazon, and all on-line music stores. I compose several different styles from hymn arrangements to meditation music, new age piano solos to pop, techno-pop, rock, and even scary Halloween music. Let me know what you think of my music!

Available on **iTunes**   Available at **amazon**   **cdbaby**

GET IT ON Google play

Available from all online music stores. Many albums are also available on Spotify and Pandora. Enjoy the music!

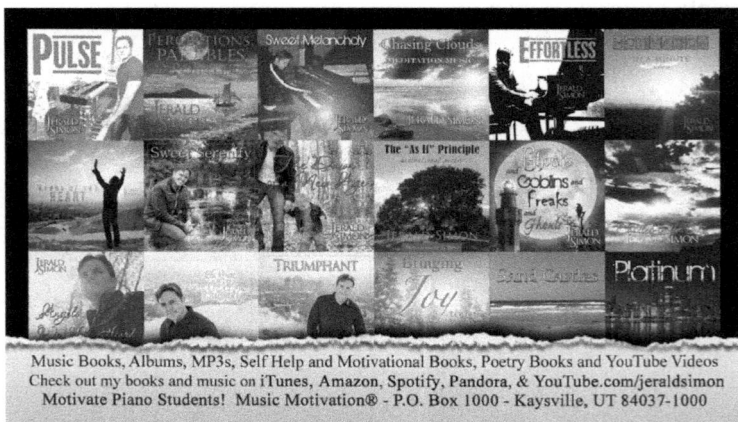

Music Books, Albums, MP3s, Self Help and Motivational Books, Poetry Books and YouTube Videos
Check out my books and music on iTunes, Amazon, Spotify, Pandora, & YouTube.com/jeraldsimon
Motivate Piano Students! Music Motivation® - P.O. Box 1000 - Kaysville, UT 84037-1000

Every month I produce and release a new **"Cool Song"** available for all piano students and piano teachers on my website (musicmotivation. com). Each new "Cool Song" is emailed to Music Motivation® mentees (piano teachers and piano students) according to their preferred subscription. See which subscription is the best fit for you and for your piano students (if you are a piano teacher) by visiting: http://musicmotivation.com/annualsubscription. I also comes out with **Theory Tip Tuesday** videos.

I have also created 25 + music books of original piano solos - most with music backing tracks of other instruments and sounds. In total there are over 250 fun piano solos between the 21 books from pre-primer to advanced level pieces that have been composed primarily to motivate teenage boys to play the piano! Purchase the PDF books at this link: **https://musicmotivation. com/product-category/pdf-downloadable-books/**

(or buy the paperback for any of these on Amazon)

Check out these best sellers by Jerald Simon

visit *musicmotivation.com* to purchase, or visit your local music store - Chesbro music is the national distributor for all Music Motivation® books. Contact Chesbro Music Co. if you are a store (1.800.243.7276)

Book Jerald as a Presenter/Performer for your next event:

Contact: Suzanne
jeraldsimon@musicmotivation.com
seminars@musicmotivation.com

Below is a list of some of the speaking and performing events Jerald has done and is willing to do.

We can customize to your specific needs.

Speaking and Performing at Events:

Workshops, Seminars, Music Camps, and Concerts (i.e. Concerts/Mini Concerts, Corporate Events/Parties/Dinners, Schools, Youth Groups, Recitals, MTNA Conventions and Conferences, MTNA Chapter Meetings, other Music Organizations, Schools, Groups, etc., Workshops, Summer Camps, Devotionals and Firesides, and any of the following:

Anniversaries, Awards Nights, Banquets, Birthday Parties, Children's Birthday Parties, Celebrations, Christmas Parties, Church Services, Clubs, Community Events, Conventions, Corporate Functions, Country Clubs, Cruise Ships, Dinner Dances, Festivals, Fund Raisers, Funerals, Graduation Parties, Grand Openings, Hotels, Jingles, Movie Sound tracks, Picnic, Private Parties, Proms, Resorts, Restaurants, Reunions, Showers, Studio Session, TV Sound tracks, Weddings, and customizable performances to meet your personal needs).

Book Jerald as the next Speaker/Entertainer for your next event! Motivate those who attend the event with Music Motivation®! Music Motivation® Workshops, Seminars, and Music Camps are focused on Theory Therapy, Innovative Improvisation, and Creative Composition with a Music Mentor. The emphasis is on teaching music students with "Music that excites, entertains, and educates". If you are interested in becoming a Music Motivation® Mentor, please email Music Motivation® at musicmentor@musicmotivation.com . If you would like to book Jerald Simon as the Music Mentor presenter or motivational speaker for your next event (i.e. recital, MTNA chapter meetings, workshops, summer camps, devotionals and firesides, corporate events, etc.) Please email Music Motivation®.

Booking Jerald is subject to his availability and waiting list.

Message to piano students from Jerald Simon...

If you come to piano lessons each week and walk away from your lessons and only learn about music notation, rhythm, and dots on a page, then I have failed as a Music Mentor. Life lessons are just as important, if not more important, than music lessons. I would rather have you learn more about goal setting and achieving, character, dedication, and personal improvement. To have you learn to love music, appreciate it, and play it, is a wonderful by-product you will have for the rest of your life - a talent that will enrich your life and the lives of others. To become a better musician is wonderful and important, but *to become a better person is more important.*

As a Music Mentor I want to mentor students to be the very best they can be. If you choose not to practice, you essentially choose not to improve. This is true in any area of life. Everyone has the same amount of time allotted to them. What you choose to do with your time, and where you spend your time, has little to do with the activities being done and more to do with the value attached to each activity.

I believe it's important to be well-rounded and have many diverse interests. I want students to enjoy music, to learn to be creative and understand how to express themselves musically - either by creating music of their own, or interpreting the music of others - by arranging and improvising well known music. In addition, I encourage students to play sports, dance, sing, draw, read, and develop their talents. I want them to be more than musicians, I want them to learn to become well-rounded complete individuals.

Above all, I want everyone to continually improve and do their best no matter what they do or choose to do. I encourage everyone to set goals, dream big, and be the best they can be in whatever they choose to do. Life is full of wonderful choices. Choose the best out of life and learn as much as you can from everyone - everywhere. I prefer being called a Music Mentor because I want to mentor others and help them to live their dreams.

Your life is your musical symphony. Make it a masterpiece!

Helping Teenagers

Want to Play the Piano with
COOL SONGS (I composed for Piano Students)

In the intro to this book I mentioned how and why I began creating what have become known as COOL SONGS. I had piano students who needed and wanted different music. The music available for them did not encourage them or motivate them enough to want to play or practice the piano. I asked my students to help me understand what kind of music they wanted so I could compose the music they wanted to play. That is how I began composing the COOL SONGS. Each one was composed for an individual student during their lesson time. Later I compiled these COOL SONGS into the COOL SONGS series (**Cool Songs for Cool Kids - Primer Level** {featuring 21 cool songs}, **Cool Songs for Cool Kids book 1** {featuring 21 cool songs}, **Cool Songs for Cool Kids book 2** {featuring 21 cool songs}, **Cool Songs for Cool Kids book 3** {featuring 10 cool songs}, and later **Cool Songs that ROCK!** book 1 {featuring 7 cool rock songs} and **Cool Songs that ROCK!** book 2 {featuring 10 cool rock songs}). After composing these 90 COOL SONGS for my own piano students - from primer level up to late intermediate levels, I continued composing more COOL SONGS at the request of piano teachers and piano students all over the world. For two years I had a monthly COOL SONGS subscription package available to piano teachers and piano students. I received their individual requests for new COOL SONGS and composed 86 additional COOL SONGS complete with backing minus tracks featuring drums, guitars, keyboards, synths, and other fun special sound effects to help teen piano students get excited about playing fun and COOL sounding music at their level.

I have since put these 86 additional COOL SONGS into three separate COOL SONGS packages:

1. Cool Songs Beginning Level,
2. Cool Songs Early Intermediate Level, and
3. Cool Songs Intermediate Level.

On the next page I include the images from my website of the three different COOL SONGS packages. I have since combined the various books from the COOL SONGS series into each of these COOL SONGS packages according to the student's level of playing ability and skill.

It has been wonderful to receive feedback from various piano teachers, piano students, and parents of piano students, from all over the world, who have started using these COOL SONGS in their piano studios. One of the main comments or feedback I receive about these COOL SONGS is how much the students enjoy playing along with the minus tracks and performing these COOL SONGS for their friends and family members. Piano teachers and parents of piano students tell me their piano students practice so much more than they used to and sometimes won't stop playing the piano because they are having so much fun playing these COOL SONGS.

Cool Songs Beginning Level
by Jerald Simon
musicmotivation.com/coolsongs

**Cool Songs Early
Intermediate Level**
by Jerald Simon
musicmotivation.com/coolsongs

Cool Songs Intermediate Level
by Jerald Simon
musicmotivation.com/coolsongs

To better help piano teachers, piano students, and parents of piano students effectively learn the music theory and what to do with that knowledge, thus bridging the gap between learning the scales and chords and using them to enhance the music, and make music of your own, I have created a course featuring step by step piano lesson videos to accompany my book:

"Essential Piano Exercises."

You can visit **ESSENTIALPIANOEXERCISES.COM** to learn more about this course and gain access to the hundreds of videos where I demonstrate how to play these exercises and then teach what you can do with them. Learning the theory is good, but knowing what to do with it is the practical application where I demonstrate how to use music theory to arrange, to improvise, to compose, and to create music of your own. More important than simply learning the theory is the practical application of *why* we are learning these scales and chords, and *what* we can do with them once we have learned them. It is the hands on approach to teaching music theory. In addition, I explain the theory in practical and simple terms so everyone can easily understand and know music theory for what it can do to help them in three primary ways: (1) sight-read the piano music better and faster as a result of knowing the scales and chords, (2) take their music playing and music creating to the next level so they can improvise, arrange, and compose music of their own, and (3) ultimately feel comfortable and excited to learn music theory - the "FUN way!"

There is more information about the Essential Piano Exercises on the next page if you would like to learn more about learning music theory, improvisation, and composition on the piano.

Join the **Essential Piano Exercises Course** by Jerald Simon

EssentialPianoExercises.com

Gain lifetime access to the following PDF books (which include video piano lesson tutorials where Jerald Simon demonstrates examples from the book and gives piano pointers, tips to try, and the practical application of music theory where Jerald demonstrates how to use the music theory!

This course features pre-recorded video lessons so you can watch and learn how to play the piano at your convenience. You choose when and where you learn to play the piano.

This Course features the following books (included as PDF downloads with the course):

1. Essential Piano Exercises Every Piano Player Should Know - PDF book and Video Course
2. 100 Left Hand Patterns Every Piano Player Should Know - PDF book and Video Course
3. Essential Jazz Piano Exercises Every Piano Player Should Know - PDF book and Video Course
4. Essential New Age Piano Exercises Every Piano Player Should Know - PDF book and Video Course
5. 100 Chord Progressions Every Piano Player Should Know - PDF book and Video Course
6. Jazzed about Jazz - PDF book and Video Course
7. Jazzed about Christmas - PDF book and Video Course
8. Jazzed about 4th of July - PDF book and Video Course
9. Fake Book FUNdamentals - Getting Started with using Fakebooks at the piano
10. Innovative Improvisation Ideas Every Piano Player Should Know - PDF book and Video Course

In addition to having access to these PDF books and Video Courses, the following will be added to you lifetime account:

- New video piano lessons are added every Monday and Friday until January 1st, 2021.
- After January 1st, 2021 new material will continue to be added on Mondays and Fridays as before, but will only be available for monthly members who have a subscription to access the new materials added each month ($29.95 per month for a monthly subscription). Anyone who has purchased the Essential Piano Exercises course will continue to have access to all of the PDF books, video lesson tutorials, power point presentations, and handouts. New books, additional MP3s, new video lessons, and monthly training seminars, webinars, and additional resources will be added for the current members of the Essential Piano Exercises monthly subscription group.
- Access to the Essential Piano Exercises Facebook group - a closed Facebook group created only for the members of the Essential Piano Exercises course. By joining the Facebook group you will have access to additional live piano lessons every week taught by Jerald Simon on Mondays at 11:00 a.m. Weekly piano pointers, tips to try, and short video lessons will be shared throughout the week for the members of the Facebook group.

Download this **FREE PDF book** -
"20 Ways to Motivate Teen Piano Students to Want to Play the Piano" at:
https://www.coolsongsclub.com/freebook.

This book includes the piano music to 30 FREE Cool Songs I have composed over the years. These COOL SONGS are the same ones used in my Cool Songs Series (without the video lessons, and MP3 minus tracks. You can learn more about my Cool Songs Series at: **https://www.coolsongsclub.com** or **https://www.musicmotivation.com**

Make the most of each minute!

This is the last page of this book, but it is the beginning of a new day for you and for me. Every day that comes our way is pure, free from mistakes, perfect. It only becomes imperfect if we allow ourselves to get in the way and mess things up. We can make the most of each minute we have by focusing on doing our best right now. Don't worry about what is on the horizon. Take it into consideration as how you can prepare right now for what is to come, but stay in the moment and enjoy everything right now.

Life is too short to get tangled up in the tragedies of tomorrow. Be happy this hour. It's a new day for change, growth, improvement, happiness, love, laughter, and giving. Every second should be sacred because they add up to more than minutes - they add up to memories. Make the most of each moment and make good memories. Make great memories. Life should be about learning and growing, but in addition to being meaningful, it should and must be memorable.

If you slip up and get down on yourself, as we all do, it's okay. Start over every second with a clean slate and a glad attitude. You can refer to it as your gladitude.

Look in the mirror and tell yourself you love yourself. Be honest and sincere and mean it. It's more than learning to like yourself, which you must do, it's about loving your strengths, accepting your weaknesses and being willing to work on them, and letting go of any unrealistic expectations of yourself. Your future is bright and beautiful, and wonderful.

Be Happy! Smile all the while and be your best!

- JERALD